Walt Disney
From Mickey to the Magic Kingdom

WALT COMMANDEERS the Ernest S. Marsh, one of the locomotives on the Santa Fe & Disneyland Railroad in 1966, the year of his death. Disney had a lifelong fascination with trains.

ERNEST S. MARSH

SANTA FE & DISNEYLAND R.R.

Walt Disney

WALT IN HIS OLDSMOBILE outside his Burbank studios in 1951. The complex was built in the late 1930s to Disney's exacting specifications, but many animators thought the state-of-the-art amenities hampered both community and creativity. "It was so nice that it was almost sterile," historian Steven Watts told PBS. "It was all rationalized. It was all organized. And something, the quality of the creative experience, was almost designed out of the operation."

FRONT COVER: Walt Disney with Mickey Mouse, circa 1930. Photograph © United Artists, courtesy Photofest

BACK COVER: Fireworks over Cinderella Castle in Florida on December 12, 2010. Photograph by Tom Bricker

MARC WANAMAKER / BISON ARCHIVES

The World of Walt Disney

By J.I. Baker

Future entrepreneurs and geniuses, take note: Despite the perception that Walt Disney's career was an unbroken series of triumphs, the great visionary arguably failed (materially, at least) more often than he succeeded. As a poor boy in Kansas City, Missouri, he delivered papers in the deep snow to help his unsuccessful father. As an ambitious young adult in the Midwest and Hollywood, he struggled with bankruptcy, borrowing money and subsisting on beans for years—until he had a hit with the Mickey Mouse cartoons in the late 1920s. (Would you believe no one wanted them at first?)

Hollywood insiders called the world's first feature-length animated film, *Snow White and the Seven Dwarfs,* "Disney's Folly"—until Walt proved them wrong when it became a worldwide hit in 1937. But three of the four Disney animated features that followed—*Pinocchio, Fantasia,* and *Bambi*—bombed. (Only *Dumbo,* a rush job, was a hit.) Though the ever-optimistic Walt kept wishing upon stars, that didn't pay the bills—and he struggled through a debilitating strike, a catastrophic war, and plenty of box-office bombs. (Where's the Blue Fairy when you need her?) But his dreams came true again in the mid-'50s when the astronomical success of Disneyland put the company in the black, erasing decades' worth of debt.

Whether Walt was riding high or suffering from what he called "the D.D.s" (disillusionment and discouragement), LIFE was there, covering everything from the first Mickey merchandising to the launch of Walt Disney World in 1971. During the studio's World War II doldrums, we published full-page storyboards from the patriotic project *Victory Through Air Power* and showed "child-friendly" (eek!) Mickey Mouse gas masks. In the 1950s, we went behind the scenes of such classic films as *Lady and the Tramp, Sleeping Beauty,* and *20,000 Leagues Under the Sea.* And long before Johnny Depp became a household name, LIFE took readers inside the launch of a Disneyland attraction called Pirates of the Caribbean.

You'll find all of these things—and much more—in the pages that follow, painting a portrait of the entrepreneur and genius whose life, like his films, began "Once upon a time..."

LIFE'S OCTOBER 15, 1971, COVER celebrates the opening of Walt Disney World in Orlando. Characters and park staff pose before Cinderella Castle, which was twice as tall as Sleeping Beauty Castle in Disneyland and contained what LIFE called "a lavish restaurant." The park's Hall of Presidents featured all (then 36!) of the American leaders, whereas Disneyland featured just one: Abraham Lincoln. And the vinyl leaves of Florida's Swiss Family Robinson Treehouse were draped with real Spanish moss.

Marceline and the Mouse

How an ambitious small-town farm boy found worldwide fame— thanks to, well, a cartoon rodent

••

DOWNTOWN MARCELINE, Missouri, on September 21, 2001, Walt Disney's 100th birthday. The unassuming town had an enormous impact on Disney, who lived there from 1906 to 1911 while his father struggled to support his family as a farmer. The place became a paradigm that Walt was constantly seeking to replicate in the likes of, say, Disneyland's Main Street, U.S.A. "It was where he first had the normal settled life that a child craves," says author and animator Stephen Cavalier.

> ## *"The trick of making things move on film is what got me."*
> —WALT DISNEY

ABOVE: WALT DISNEY'S mother, Flora, and father, Elias, shown in the late 19th century. Whereas Walt (opposite, at age one) was ebullient and playful, Elias was stern and dour. He did not smoke or drink (Walt did plenty of both) and the only thing he did "for fun" was play the fiddle. But Walt turned fun into an empire, seemingly searching for a boyhood he never had.

n 1906, an unsuccessful carpenter named Elias Disney moved his wife, Flora, and their five children from Chicago to the town of Marceline, Missouri, hoping to find success as a farmer. Little more than a whistle-stop between the Windy City and Kansas City, Marceline was then—as now—an unlikely source of inspiration for the artist who would almost single-handedly transform American popular culture in the 20th century. But every great man was a boy once—and the Disneys' youngest son, Walt, was not quite five years old when he fell in love with the little town.

Born in Chicago on December 5, 1901, Walt would come to see Marceline as the source of the only real childhood he ever had. He spent his four short years there prowling its main street, marveling at the locomotives, and sketching the animals that populated the family farm. It was "the most important part of Walt's life," his wife, Lillian, later said. And it would exert an enduring influence on nearly everything he did—from homey films like *Pollyanna* to Disneyland's Main Street, U.S.A.

But times were hard, and Elias was not cut out for farming. In 1911, he uprooted his family and moved to Kansas City, Missouri, where the increasingly bitter man was reduced to running a paper route. His principle employees were, not surprisingly, his sons. Little Walt would rise in the predawn darkness and work all day—often in freezing cold and snow so deep it sometimes reached his neck. Now and then he fell asleep, exhausted, in apartment foyers.

But the beleaguered boy nurtured grand dreams—most of which involved escaping his often violent father, who once tried to attack him with a hammer. "Where Elias was somber and dogged, Walt was energetic and, above all, optimistic," Michael Barrier, author of *The Animated Man: A Life of Walt Disney*, tells LIFE. Walt loved attention, briefly flirting with the idea of being an actor, but he was increasingly obsessed with drawing—in part because it provided an escape from his grim home life.

In 1918, after the Allies defeated the Germans in World War I's second battle of the Marne, the patriotic Walt "just had to get in there," he said. Stationed with the Red Cross Ambulance Corps in Neufchâteux, France, the 16-year-old experienced his first taste of independence. He also

started chain-smoking, a habit that probably hastened the end of his life.

In the aftermath of the war, Walt was a young man on the make in an America flush with optimism and cash. After briefly partnering in business with fellow cartoonist Ub Iwerks—who would play a significant part in the Disney history—Walt found a job at the Kansas City Slide Company. The outfit produced crude live-action and cartoon advertisements, but the work sparked something in the ambitious teenager. "The trick of making things move on film is what got me," he later said.

Only two decades old in 1920, "animation was primitive and ramshackle," Stephen Cavalier, author of *The World History of Animation* and owner of Spy Pictures, an animation company, tells LIFE. "You could compare it to computers before Bill Gates and Steve Jobs came along." But with the instincts of a visionary artist, Walt sensed the medium's potential. Talking his boss into loaning him a camera, Walt started making his own animated films in his father's garage on nights and weekends. "Long after everyone else was [in] bed, Walt was out there still, puttering away, working away,

TEENAGE WALT is seen at left as a World War I Red Cross ambulance driver in 1918. Though he was underage, the patriotic boy had falsified his papers to join the war effort. Below: Portrait of the Artist as a Young Animator: Walt in the 1920s—probably in Kansas City, Missouri, where the ambitious teen returned after the war. There, his humble first ambition to be a newspaper cartoonist was sidelined when he fell in love with animation.

experimenting, trying this and that," his older brother Roy later said.

At the tender age of 20, Walt once again partnered with Iwerks—this time, to start his own company, Laugh-O-gram Films, notably producing a short about Alice, a live-action girl who interacted with cartoon worlds. But when this venture failed, the young man—like so many others at the time—went west,

joining Roy in Los Angeles.

"I packed all of my worldly goods—a pair of trousers, a checkered coat, a lot of drawing materials, and the last of the fairy-tale reels we had made—in a kind of frayed cardboard suitcase," Walt said later. "And with that wonderful audacity of youth, I went to Hollywood, arriving there with just 40 dollars."

The young man found little

opportunity at first. "Cartoons in the 1920s were very much an afterthought in the Hollywood scheme of things," says Barrier. But it wasn't long before Disney was asked by New York–based producer Margaret Winkler to create more Alice comedies. So Walt and Roy joined forces, with Roy the steady voice of fiscal responsibility to Walt's obsessive, sometimes reckless visionary.

MONDADORI PORTFOLIO/GETTY

WALT WITH HIS WIFE, the former Lillian Bounds, outside his Kingswell Avenue studio in the 1920s, above. At right: A poster for one of Disney's early "Alice in Cartoonland" shorts, which featured the adventures of a live-action girl in an animated world—a technique that would reach its apex in 1964's *Mary Poppins*. Opposite page: Oswald the Lucky Rabbit was Disney's first attempt to create an iconic cartoon animal. He was devastated when the creation was taken from him.

ONLINE USA/GETTY

Setting up shop in their uncle's garage on Kingswell Avenue in Los Angeles, the Disneys began pumping out shorts—and soon began to hire animators and expand, moving into a storefront on Kingswell.

In 1926, the brothers and their staff moved into a new space on Hyperion Avenue. "Like all cartoon makers [Disney] was on the lookout for a distinctive animal," LIFE magazine reported. Determined to invent a cartoon character that would rival the popularity of Felix the Cat, Walt and his team came up with Oswald the Lucky Rabbit. The new creature was mostly drawn by Iwerks, who had joined the Disneys in L.A.—and who was, Walt believed, far more talented than *he* was. ("I never did a drawing I liked," Walt once confessed.)

But just as it seemed the Disneys' luck was on the upswing, Winkler's new husband, Charles Mintz, who contractually owned Oswald, announced that he was taking the character from Walt. Not only that: He was poaching several key animators from Disney.

A massive blow, yes, but Walt always worked best under pressure. Now he and his team, determined to top both Oswald and Felix, devoured magazines, advertisements, and films seeking inspiration for a new character. Before long, they developed a creature that Iwerks characterized thusly: "Pear-shaped body, ball on top, couple of thin legs. You gave it long ears and it was a rabbit. Short ears, it was a cat. Ears hanging down a dog … With an elongated nose, it became a mouse."

Walt called the new creation "Mortimer Mouse," but Lillian Bounds, the studio worker who had become Mrs. Walt Disney in 1925, reportedly thought the moniker was "too sissy."

Instead, she suggested "Mickey."

BUYENLARGE/GETTY

Mickey Makes His

How one black-and-white cartoon (less than eight minutes long!)
changed cinema with sound—and gave birth to an empire

Mark

THOUGH MICKEY MOUSE began as Walt's alter ego—an irrepressible, optimistic, rebellious creation whose pluck resonated with Americans mired in the Great Depression—it wasn't long before he became a bland corporate mascot. His image evolved, but his character did not—despite the fact that Walt was trying to keep him relevant with such projects as *The Sorcerer's Apprentice* (third from left). Though Walt was the original voice of Mickey, he eventually gave it up—perhaps because his chain-smoking had made falsetto impossible.

> *"I had a helluva breakdown...*
> *I got to a point that I couldn't talk*
> *on the telephone. I'd begin to cry."*
> —WALT DISNEY

THE 1928 MICKEY MOUSE short *Plane Crazy* (above) was co-written and directed by Walt and his secret weapon: Ub Iwerks (seen opposite). The animator who was largely responsible for creating the look of both Oswald the Lucky Rabbit and Mickey Mouse, Iwerks had worked with Walt in Kansas City, Missouri. Shy and retiring where his partner was outgoing and aggressive, Iwerks was by far the better artist—even Walt admitted that.

The plucky little rodent's beginnings were, like Walt's, nothing if not scrappy. "The first Mickey Mouse was made by 12 people after hours in a garage," Walt later wrote. (Once again, Iwerks did the defining drawing.) Though the team quickly produced three Mickey shorts, the tyro talent could not find a distributor. Out of sheer desperation, Walt hit upon a characteristically risky idea: sound.

In 1926, the upstart Warner Brothers studio, seeking to establish itself, released *Don Juan* with a prerecorded score and sound effects. Though a hit, the film did not revolutionize the industry. But one year later, a film called *The Jazz Singer* did, becoming a sensation by incorporating its singular star Al Jolson's dialogue into the drama. "Even then, many in the industry considered quality sound technology an expensive and risky fad," says Cavalier.

Walt was not among them. "He put all his resources into the development of sound cartoons," adds Cavalier. "On the one hand, he was always driven by the fear of financial insecurity, but when he believed passionately about something, he was willing to take great risks."

Cartoons had used sound before, but Disney hadn't— and *Steamboat Willie* was unique in that its sound was synchronized, thanks to a system designed by Walt and his colleague Wilfred Jackson. "The sound effects seem to originate in what the characters are doing on the screen, and the action moves to the musical beat," says Barrier. "By contrast, the earliest cartoon sound was essentially just pasted on with no organic relationship to the visuals."

When *Steamboat Willie* premiered on November 18, 1928, at the Colony Theater in New York City (ahead of a now-forgotten film called *Gang War*), it became a sensation, making Mickey Mouse a worldwide star. "Everybody liked Mickey," LIFE reported, "the children who thought he was funny, the philosophers who thought he represented America's raucous individualism, the aesthetes who saw in him the first successful adjustment of linear design to the fluttering motion of the films."

Almost overnight, Felix the Cat found himself in the

STEAMBOAT WILLIE **(1928) was the first cartoon that used sound as a true complement to the visuals. For instance, a goat becomes a music box when Minnie Mouse turns its tail. The Mickey Mouse film became an instant smash, but it wasn't long before its star lost the impetuous quality that had made him famous.**

doghouse—and Oswald had disappeared down the rabbit hole.

In October 1929, the American stock market collapsed, erasing $140 billion in funds virtually overnight. But the Great Depression that followed was, some have said, the best thing that ever happened to Walt Disney. For one thing, it meant that talented artists desperately needed jobs. So Walt went on a hiring spree—and kept "plussing," his word for constant improvement. "He instigated programs to distill great drawing and design into simple but beautiful and expressive lines and shapes," says Cavalier.

He also hired noted artists and thinkers—among them the architect Frank Lloyd Wright—to give lectures at the studio, driving his team on to ever greater excellence. "We saw every ballet, we saw every film," said animator Marc Davis. "If a film was good, we would go and see it five times."

Walt was industrializing the animation process without killing the artistry, notes Cavalier. "He and his people analyzed the characteristics of movement, human and animal—the way living creatures move when they are feeling particular emotions," he says. In the process, Walt transformed the medium from a vehicle for crude gags to what became known as character animation. "It was no longer just moving things—it was real acting with real emotion."

Walt and Roy approached the Disney art as pure product, too. "The merchandising business began in an offhand way in 1930," LIFE reported, "when somebody paid Walt $300 for the right to put Mickey ... on a line of stationery."

Before long, there were Mickey Mouse lunch boxes, playing cards, bridge favors, candy, watering cans, and soap (just to name a few), and the Mickey Mouse watch became the most popular timepiece in America. "When some explorers hacked their way through the least penetrable jungle of Brazil, the first little boy to greet

them was wearing a Mickey Mouse sweater," LIFE reported.

As Walt's success grew and he kept hiring, his employees became surrogate sons. (He called them his "boys.") Increasingly, he viewed the studio as the home that he had never had. "His drive to achieve, the success and financial security he craved, and his obsession with family—family entertainment, family values, a family atmosphere at his studio—stemmed from his childhood insecurities," says Cavalier.

But Walt was more like his father than he wanted to believe—and, like Elias, he had a temper, often lashing out at his "boys," according to biographer Neal Gabler. (One of them was "Friz" Freleng, who would later help create the iconic *Looney Tunes* franchise at Warner Brothers. "He became abusive and harassed me," Freleng said.)

Still, Walt had a knack for inspiring his people with his enthusiasms, leading them all to believe—as he did—that their work was a calling, a mission, even a religion. "We'd hate to go home at night," said Iwerks, "and we couldn't wait to get to the office in the morning." But no one worked harder than Walt, who virtually lived at the studio—a fact that sometimes led to tension at home.

"I love Mickey Mouse more than any woman I've ever known," Walt once told animator Ward Kimball. Indeed, Lillian told *Time* magazine she was "a mouse widow," claiming that her husband only ever talked

Mickey Mouse floats down New York City's Broadway in the 1934 Macy's Thanksgiving Day Parade. "Mickey Mouse would have been fame enough for most men," the *New York Times* wrote in Walt's obituary. "In France he was known as Michel Souris; in Italy, Topolino; in Japan, Miki Kuchi; in Spain, Miguel Ratoncito; in Latin America, El Raton Miguelito; in Sweden, Muse Pigg, and in Russia, Mikki Maus."

about his alter ego, Mickey. When Walt was hailed as a "genius," Lillian responded: "Try living with one." Still, their bond was real and enduring.

In 1931, Disney's domestic situation seemed about to change when Lillian became pregnant. Child-loving Walt was thrilled. But her miscarriage—combined with Walt's ever-increasing workload—led to "a helluva breakdown," he later said. "I went all to pieces. Costs were going up; I was always way over what they figured the pictures would bring in ... I just got very irritable. I got to a point that I couldn't talk on the telephone. I'd begin to cry."

Following doctor's orders, Walt took his first vacation, traveling across the country with Lillian. "I had the time of my life," he said. "It was actually the first time we had ever been away on anything like that since we were married."

Returning refreshed and rejuvenated, Walt followed his doctor's advice by adding exercise to his routine, often rising at 5:30 a.m. to play golf in Griffith Park. But he remained a driven workaholic—a fact that didn't change when, in 1933, the Disneys finally welcomed a daughter, Diane. In 1937 they adopted a second daughter, Sharon.

Walt doted on his children—maybe even more so than the comparatively reserved Lillian did—but his work consumed him, and he often missed their birthdays. Though he rarely had leisure time, Walt started hobnobbing with the Hollywood

Continued on page 26

SELECTIONS FROM ZAMPA

THE BAND CONCERT, the first Mickey Mouse film in color, circa 1935, was the inspiration—decades later—for Silly Symphony Swings, an attraction at Disney California Adventure Park. Walt was the first to use Technicolor in commercial films—beginning with 1932's Silly Symphony *Flowers and Trees.* Because no one was sure how audiences would react to the new technology, the short was simultaneously produced in black and white. But the premiere of the color version at Grauman's Chinese Theatre caused a sensation.

WALT AND HIS WIFE, Lillian, in 1933, above. Opposite: Walt was not much given to relaxation or recreation, but in the 1930s he embraced the Hollywood vogue for polo, even creating a 1936 short called *Mickey's Polo Team*, in which the mouse competes with the likes of Laurel and Hardy, Harpo Marx, and Charlie Chaplin.

envy of every animator—if not film-maker—in the world.

But they were more than merely aesthetic. Always "plussing," Walt used the Symphonies to test new technical developments—such as Technicolor (1932's *Flowers and Trees*, the first cartoon to win an Oscar) and the multiplane camera (a device that created an unprecedented illusion of realism and depth) in 1937's *The Old Mill*, which won yet another Oscar.

But the Silly Symphony highlight was the sophisticated character animation that fueled 1933's *The Three Little Pigs*. "Nothing like this had been seen in earlier cartoons, where the intent was not to bring characters to life but to slide by with as few drawings as possible," says Barrier. Even the hypercritical Walt knew it: "At last we have achieved true personality in a whole picture!" he said.

The Three Little Pigs and its iconic song, "Who's Afraid of the Big, Bad Wolf?" became a sensation in the midst of the Depression. (It was the first cartoon tune to become a hit.) But "you can't top pigs with pigs," Walt said—even as he remained determined to top himself.

"In the 1920s, Disney met a stranger on a train who was interested to hear that he produced motion pictures," says Cavalier. "But when Disney told him that he made cartoons, the man lost interest. This is the kind of attitude that riled Disney and drove him, for a while at least, to make something more grown-up and serious and respected."

Nothing Walt had ever done—or arguably ever would—was as "grown-up and serious and respected" as his next project. Though the idea had been percolating for years, in the spring of 1933 Walt called his employees into the Hyperion soundstage. There, he sat in a spotlight and, for several hours, did what he did best.

He told a story.

elite—mostly through the then-faddish sport of polo. But polo was not without hazards: a fellow player died in 1935, and Walt himself suffered a neck injury that would trouble him for the rest of his life.

In 1929, with the release of *The Skeleton Dance*, Walt inaugurated a new cartoon series called Silly Symphonies. "We wanted a series which would let us go in for more of the fantastic and fabulous and lyric stuff," Walt said. Using music to drive the animation rather than merely augment it, these nearly avant-garde shorts went far beyond anything that had ever been done, making the Disney Studios the

The Big Five

How the first feature-length cartoon, Snow White and the Seven Dwarfs, *led to an unprecedented run of classic films… and unforeseen failure*

• •

CROWDS GATHER OUTSIDE the Carthay Circle Theatre on January 30, 1941, for the premiere of *Fantasia*. The third film of the studio's so-called Big Five, it was a box-office flop. But it enjoyed a countercultural (not to say chemical) revival in the 1970s, with LIFE's William Zinsser calling Disney "a hippie 30 years ahead of his time, producing a psychedelic light-and-sound show that was his only flop because nobody was freaked out enough to dig it."

> ## "We'd sometimes take a whole day for a closeup of Snow White."
> —ANIMATOR ROBERT GIVENS

n January 1917, a silent film version of the Grimms' fairy tale "Snow White" was shown at the Kansas City, Missouri, convention hall, making a particularly big impact on one 16-year-old boy in the gallery. "My impression of the picture has stayed with me through the years," Walt later wrote, "and I know it played a big part in selecting *Snow White* for my first feature production."

Two decades after that screening, Walt mesmerized his Hyperion audience with his vision of a feature-length cartoon version of the fairy tale. "The way that boy can tell a story is nobody's business," one colleague said. "I was practically in tears during some of it. If it should turn out one tenth as good as the way he tells it, it should be a wow."

But mounting such an ambitious—and risky— production would require plenty of cash. Unable to secure Hollywood financing, the Disneys turned to Bank of America, which eventually loaned the studio a good portion of the film's $1.5 million budget.

Following time-honored tradition, the filmmakers first approached the story by focusing on gags, but these were increasingly sidelined in favor of character development and realism. Even more than *The Three Little Pigs, Snow White and the Seven Dwarfs* would show that Walt and his "boys" had mastered the ability to make an animated character's inner life visible. "Whatever passes through, say, Grumpy's mind is simultaneously visible in his face and body," says Barrier. This was the ultimate in character animation.

Using *The Old Mill's* technical innovations, *Snow White* attained unprecedented realism and depth through the use of the multiplane camera. The effects were breathtaking, but the device added many hours of work to a film that would involve two million drawings. "We'd sometimes take a whole day for a closeup of Snow White," animator Robert Givens told PBS. "That's how intricate the drawing was."

Walt drove his animators with characteristic perfectionism, scrutinizing every image and gesture. (He was obsessed with the size of one of Grumpy's fingers, for

PROVIDING THE VOICE and image of Snow White, 18-year-old Adriana Caselotti (right, with an animator) said she had no idea that she was working on a feature film. "They had told me that it was going to be a little longer than their shorts, which were 10 to 12 minutes," said Caselotti, who was paid $970 for her work. "I didn't realize what had happened until I went to the premiere. I saw all these movie stars—Marlene Dietrich, Carole Lombard, Gary Cooper— everybody was there. I discovered this thing was an hour and 23 minutes."

instance, and he once complained that the wicked Queen looked like "she was carrying a big load of laundry.") In the end, though every detail had been endlessly rehashed, Walt insisted that the film should feel, more than anything else, *spontaneous*. "He was a real micromanager," says Cavalier, "maybe because his fear of failure came from that precarious home life of his childhood."

Walt may have inherited his father's restlessness and something of his temper, but he hadn't inherited Elias's thrift. "I've only thought of money in one way, and that is to do something with it, you see?" he once said. Now *Snow White*'s budget kept increasing as more and more people were added to the payroll.

Even so, the studio was behind schedule. The huge amount of time that had gone into preliminary planning and tinkering meant that, only 10 months before the December premiere, most of the film had yet to be animated. Rumors spread that Disney wouldn't make the deadline,

fueling the press's characterization of the project as Disney's Folly.

Even when the film was nearly finished, Walt could not stop obsessing over imperfections: In the last scene, for instance, Prince Charming shimmied. A horrified Walt was determined to correct it, but the money had run out. "Let the Prince shimmy!" Roy declared. (The odd motion was eventually corrected.)

Now it was time to introduce *Snow White* to the world. Though Walt knew his team had created something special, he also knew the film wouldn't work if it didn't deliver a complete emotional journey. Would the audience be able to suspend disbelief during nearly 90 minutes of an animated film? Would they be moved when Snow White "dies," having eaten the Queen's poison apple?

The premiere was held on December 21, 1937, at L.A.'s prestigious Carthay Circle Theatre. Sure enough, the audience laughed— and they were frightened by Snow

SCENES FROM A CLASSIC, opposite, clockwise from top left: Snow White with Dopey; the Queen with a box designed to hold Snow White's heart; and the film's all-important scene: the dwarfs mourning Snow White. (If this scene didn't work, Disney knew the movie wouldn't either. Needless to say, it worked.) Top: Walt accepts his honorary Oscar (and seven tiny ones) from Shirley Temple. He thought he deserved the award for Best Picture, but the honor dubiously went to *The Life of Emile Zola*.

TECHNICIANS IN THE DISNEY sound production room record effects in 1938, when *Pinocchio, Fantasia,* and *Bambi* were all in the works following the success of *Snow White.* "Technologically Disney wasn't really a pioneer," says animator and author Stephen Cavalier, "but he took inventions like the multiplane camera and sound technology and even animation itself and refined them so they really worked well, in a slick and commercial and aesthetically appealing way."

White's flight through the forest and the transformation of the Queen into the evil crone. But the crucial question—would they cry?—was more than answered when the dwarfs mourned the seemingly dead Snow White. The audience of Hollywood insiders sniffled audibly—none more so than Clark Gable and Carole Lombard.

When the film ended, the audience erupted into a standing ovation.

The critics applauded, too. *Time* magazine presciently called *Snow White* "an authentic masterpiece, to be shown in theaters and beloved by new generations long after the current crop of Hollywood stars, writers, and directors are sleeping where no Prince's kiss can wake them." The picture was, in short, a triumph, quickly becoming the most successful American film ever made up to that point, earning eight million dollars in its first release. It proved just as popular overseas, where people had to reserve seats three weeks in advance.

Snow White became the first female fictional character to be given a star on the Hollywood Walk of Fame (Mickey, of course, had been the first male character), and that February Walt received an honorary Oscar, presented by Shirley Temple: one normal-size statuette attached to seven smaller ones. "I'm so proud I think I'll bust," Walt said, though he was privately miffed that his breakthrough hadn't been nominated for Best

W.D.P.
701-1

MARC WANAMAKER/BISON ARCHIVES

© WALT DISNEY PRODUCTIONS, COURTESY PHOTOFEST

WALT WORKS THOUGH a scene from *Pinocchio*, the studio's second animated feature, top. Though many think the film is an even greater achievement than *Snow White*, it was beset with problems, chief of which was: How do you make a wooden puppet both believable and sympathetic? The answer: Pair him with a talking cricket (above). Opposite page: Walt's approach to parenthood was the polar opposite of his distant father's. Here, he tells daughters Diane and Sharon the story of Pinocchio.

Picture. (He would have to wait nearly three decades for that honor, but he has won more Academy Awards than anyone in history.)

Almost overnight, the Disney studio was flush, its creditors paid off. But after spending the better part of three years supervising every detail on *Snow White*, Walt now found himself the head of a studio that was expected to produce product on a regular basis. His stated goal was to produce a picture every six months, but how do you do that when your exacting eye endlessly examines every detail?

Tragedy got in the way, too. In 1938, Walt and Roy gave their proud parents a home in North Hollywood as a 50th-anniversary present. But the structure had a faulty heating system—and, on November 16, Flora Disney died of carbon monoxide poisoning. Walt never spoke of the calamity, dealing with his grief the only way he knew how: He went back to work.

The first order of business was finding a follow-up to *Snow White*. It was supposed to be *Bambi*, the animated version of the Felix Salten novel, but when Walt decided that the story was too complicated, he shifted his focus to *Pinocchio*. That, too, presented problems. In Carlo Collodi's classic Italian folktale, Pinocchio is crude and often cruel—killing the character who would become, in Disney's version, Jiminy Cricket.

Far from dying, the cartoon Jiminy proved the key to humanizing the puppet, serving as the film's narrator and Pinocchio's conscience—not to mention the inspiration for the song "When You Wish Upon a Star," which came to represent the entire Disney brand.

Given Walt's mind-set at the time, the tune might as well have been called "Be Careful What You Wish For." He was beginning to worry that he'd lost control of his empire, according to Gabler—feelings that were embodied in the new Mickey Mouse short, *The Sorcerer's Apprentice*, set to Paul Dukas's composition of the same name. Was Walt himself the Sorcerer, wielding the power that allowed him to produce unparalleled wonders? Or was he Mickey, a novice dabbling in magic that he was ultimately unable to control?

Originally an attempt to keep a marginalized Mickey relevant, the short pleased Walt so much that, even with *Pinocchio* in progress, he decided to include it in a project

EARL THEISEN/GETTY

RIGHT: WALT (FAR LEFT) watches an animator at work on *Fantasia* as conductor Leopold Stokowski (center) and narrator Deems Taylor (second from right) look on in 1940. Below: Luminescent jellyfish reflect the beginnings of life on earth in *Fantasia*'s *Rite of Spring* segment. Bottom and opposite page: *Fantasia* began as a short called *The Sorcerer's Apprentice,* Walt's attempt to give the increasingly marginalized Mickey something to do.

that he called the Concert Feature. He was particularly inspired by meetings with the celebrity conductor Leopold Stokowski, who had been so impressed by *The Sorcerer's Apprentice* that he agreed to conduct the music gratis. The men soon spent months together selecting classical music that Walt thought could be successfully animated.

The Concert Feature was wildly ambitious—not least because it was being produced at the same time as *Pinocchio* and *Bambi*. But Walt had other plans, too. Knowing that his rapidly expanding empire had outgrown the Hyperion studio, he purchased 51 acres in Burbank in 1938.

Typically, Walt threw himself into planning the new space, putting as much effort and enthusiasm—not to mention money—into the project as he did into any of his films. The studio would feature a theater, restaurant, private club, soda fountain, cafeteria, gas station, recreation spaces, and—crucially—air conditioning. (When temperatures rose in Los Angeles, sweat stained the animators' drawings.)

But Walt was about to experience a financial double whammy.

In February 1940, *Pinocchio* premiered to rave reviews—many

critics thought it was an even greater achievement than *Snow White*—but it proved a commercial disappointment. (Walt blamed the failure on the recent release of *Gone with the Wind*, though the war raging in Europe certainly had something to do with it.)

That same November, the Concert Feature was released as *Fantasia* to mixed reviews: Walt had cheapened the classics, some said, and had turned Igor Stravinsky's controversial *Rite of Spring*—about pagan Russian rituals—into a dumb dinosaur diorama. (Stravinsky himself called it "an unresisting imbecility.") Though Stokowski himself had argued against including Beethoven's *Pastoral* Symphony, saying that the master was "worshipped," Walt held his ground, doing himself no favors by saying, "I think this thing will make Beethoven."

Of course, *Fantasia* is now considered a classic—and it later enjoyed a

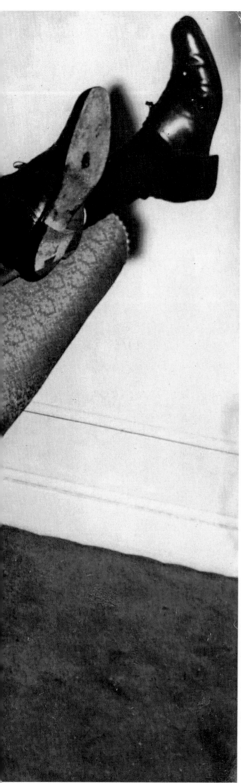

WALT STUDIES MUSICAL
scores in 1938, left. Even when
he was relaxing, he was
working. Below: Though many
refer to a "Disney look," the
studio's first five features are all
visually distinct. The simple
lines and colors of *Dumbo*
(below) have nothing in
common with the realistic,
painterly effects of *Bambi,* for
instance. Walt never took
Dumbo that seriously, but it was
the studio's first animated
feature hit since *Snow White*.

druggie revival among countercul-
ture youths. (In 1970, LIFE's William
Zinsser called it "America's first acid
happening.") But it proved an even
bigger commercial disappointment
than *Pinocchio*—in part because Walt
insisted on the use of Fantasound, an
expensive sound system that many
theaters were unequipped to handle.

Clearly quick fixes were needed.

Since live action was cheaper
than animation, Walt rushed *The
Reluctant Dragon* (which combined
the two) into production. Hosted by
Robert Benchley, 1941's behind-the-
scenes tour of the Disney studios was
surprisingly effective but fell short of
breaking even.

With *Bambi* still inching intermi-
nably forward, Walt found another
animation project that could be
made fast and on the cheap, calling
it "Just one of those little things that
we knocked out between epics!" But

WALT SKETCHES 12-week-old fawns that are the models for the hero and heroine of 1942's *Bambi* (left). Disney photographers and artists recorded the bodies and actions of the animals as they grew, bringing accuracy to a film about the life cycle of a deer. Above: *Bambi* balances unprecedented realism—and emotional darkness—with the cuteness shown here as Bambi pals around with Thumper the rabbit and Flower the skunk.

1941's *Dumbo* became the most successful animated picture the studio had produced since *Snow White*—and the *New York Times* called it "the most genial, the most endearing, the most completely precious cartoon feature film ever to emerge from the magical brushes of Walt Disney's wonder-working artists!"

Bambi was another story. A much greater (and subtler) technical achievement than *Dumbo,* it bombed when it was released in 1942. It was also savaged by critics, one of whom called it "entirely unpleasant." Even Walt's daughter Diane was unhappy, asking her father why Bambi's mother had to die. "Life is composed of lights and shadows," Walt later explained, giving the lie to those who complain that his work was nothing but pap, "and we would be untruthful, insincere, and saccharine if we tried to pretend there were no shadows."

Known as the Big Five, Disney's sublime first run of animated films (made over six years) has never been equaled. But the studio was losing money; many felt the magic had gone, and—crucially—Walt's "boys" had turned against their paterfamilias.

Trouble in Toonland

How two crises— a crippling strike and the Second World War— changed the Disney studio (and Walt himself) forever

• •

WALT IN HIS OFFICE IN 1944. Although the studio was requisitioned for the war effort and generated several films for the U.S. government, the 1940s were not kind to Disney, and he wouldn't truly hit his innovative, lucrative stride again until Disneyland in the '50s. We tend to think of Walt as going from one success to another, but—like many artists and entrepreneurs—his triumphs were punctuated by failures.

"I have a case of the D.D.s—
disillusionment and discouragement."
—WALT DISNEY

When the Great Depression ended in 1939, millions of American workers, having endured years of unemployment, began demanding job security and a stake in the new prosperity, leading to a radicalism that influenced labor relations—not least in the movie business.

By 1940, Hollywood's Screen Cartoonists Guild had unionized the town's major animation departments except Disney's, despite the fact that the Mouse House employed the vast majority of the industry's artists.

There was little consistency in Disney studio salaries or perks. The most valued animators were allowed entrance to the so-called Penthouse Club, which included a steam room and a gym featuring a personal trainer who had competed on the Swedish Olympic team. But "lesser" artists often couldn't afford to eat in the cafeteria. To make matters worse, the Disney organization reluctantly went public in 1940, selling stock to meet its mounting losses.

Suddenly employees knew what the boss was making: at least five times that of his top people. And the women in the lowly Ink and Paint Department (one of the few places where women were allowed) were paid a pittance. "Walt was following a very hard-line capitalist model," says Stephen Cavalier: "the big boss upstairs with the vision, and the worker drones down on the production line."

Increasingly dissatisfied, Disney's workers moved toward unionization. For Walt, this was literally unbelievable: Weren't they all a family? In February 1941, he held a meeting he thought would resolve the issue once and for all. Instead, he inflamed it. "My first recommendation to the lot of you is this," he said: "Put your own house in order ... If you're not progressing as you should, instead of grumbling and growling, do something about it."

This condescending speech turned even more Disney employees to the union cause than before. On May 29, 1941, after a valued senior animator named Art Babbitt was fired for joining the union, nearly half the Disney art department walked out. Even as the studio's stock dropped precipitously because its films were losing money, Walt refused to negotiate. In fact, when Babbitt shouted from the picket

THE WALT DISNEY STUDIO in Burbank in 1942 (opposite, top). Opposite, bottom: In 1940, color artists touch up studio signage. Virtually a self-contained city, the new studio was something of a dry run for Disneyland, featuring some of the same innovations, such as tunnels connecting the buildings and its own sewage system. This page: An "inker" works on *Pinocchio*. This is pretty much the only job that women were allowed to do. Not surprisingly, they were paid far less than the men.

MEMBERS OF THE SCREEN
Cartoonists Guild picket the
Disney Studios in Burbank on
May 28, 1941. "Disney felt like
his generals, his apostles, his
brothers had betrayed him,"
says animator and author
Stephen Cavalier. "Those
strikes and the high-brow
critics' scorn at *Fantasia*
wounded him, killed off a part
of him, and tempered his
passion for his films."

line, "Shame on you, Walt Disney!" as
Walt drove to work, Disney got out of
his car and charged at him.

Disheartened and confused, Walt
fell back on a paranoid conspiracy
theory, claiming through an ad in the
trade paper *Variety* that the strike was
"Communistic." But he was, for once,
powerless. "Animators were highly
skilled workers, hard to replace
with scabs, which provided them
with added leverage," Gerald Horne,
author of *Class Struggle in Hollywood:
1930–1950,* tells LIFE.

Just as he had done after his ner-
vous breakdown, Walt escaped—this
time, to South America. "It gives
me a chance to get away from this
god-awful nightmare," he wrote. "I
have a case of the D.D.s—disillusionment and discouragement."

During Walt's southern sojourn,
his father, Elias, died. Disney did
not return for the funeral, but
when he finally reemerged in Los
Angeles, Walt discovered that Roy
had resolved the strike. But nothing would ever be the same—not
least because on December 7, 1941,
the Japanese bombed Pearl Harbor,
sending a shocked America reeling
into World War II.

From the start, Walt's perspec-
tive on the conflict had been
uninformed. (When asked
how the war might affect the
studio, he replied: "What war?") But
after half the studio was requisitioned
as a base for antiaircraft troops, Walt
threw himself into making government training and propaganda films.

Continued on page 53

WALT FILMING on a Brazilian beach. During the strike against his studio, he went to South America on a government-sponsored "goodwill" trip. He thought the journey might "bring back some extra work into the plant"—and it did lead to little-known wartime films like *Saludos Amigos* and *The Three Caballeros*. A steamer ride that Walt took into a Colombian rain forest may have inspired the Jungle Cruise at Disneyland.

OPPOSITE PAGE: Lieutenant J.C. Hutchison, left, and Walt examine a model plane in front of sketches for a naval flight training film. This page, at left: Walt hands his sketch of a Mickey Mouse gas mask to Major General William Porter, right, in Washington in 1942. (The design was intended to appeal to children, reminding them to use their masks!) Below left: Donald Duck dreams he's a Nazi in 1943's Oscar-winning *Der Fuehrer's Face*.

(The most popular was arguably *Der Fuehrer's Face*, in which Donald Duck dreams he's working in a German munitions factory.)

Walt found little creative satisfaction in this work, but some of his old enthusiasm returned with the making of 1943's *Victory Through Air Power*, based on a 1942 nonfiction book that aviation aficionado Walt had become enamored with. (At one point in the film, an animated woman is shown reading a copy of LIFE at the beautician's, saying, "Jeepers! The President wants 50,000 planes a year!")

Victory was, however, a flop, and the studio made slim profits from its government endeavors. After the war ended in 1945, the cash-strapped Walt announced: "We're through with caviar. From now on it's mashed potatoes and gravy." Desperately needing a hit, Walt returned to his Marceline paradigm, focusing on folksy Americana instead of European folktales in a little picture called *Song of the South*.

Based on the Uncle Remus stories by Joel Chandler Harris, the film was set in the South in the late 1800s. Initially concerned that it might seem racially insensitive, Walt solicited the input of black leaders, who warned him against featuring, for instance, happy slaves singing songs.

But Walt followed his own instincts—and the finished film did show happy black sharecroppers singing songs. ("Let the rain pour down! Let the cold wind blow!

ZIP-A-DEE DOO-DAH

Walt Disney's **Song of the South**

TECHNICOLOR® G ALL AGES ADMITTED

WALT WATCHES as musician Johnny Mercer plays music from 1946's notorious *Song of the South* (above). Soon after, Mercer had a Top 10 single with the film's "Zip-a-Dee-Doo-Dah," which was based on the song "Zip Coon," popularized by 19th-century blackface performers—a popular form of entertainment now considered racist. Some lyrics: "O zip a duden duden zip a duden day." Opposite: Walt testifies in 1947 before the House Un-American Activities Committee in Washington.

Gonna stay right here in the home I know!") To make matters worse, the film's November premiere was held in Atlanta, Georgia, which remained segregated, meaning that James Baskett, who played Uncle Remus, could not get a hotel room.

Instead of the comeback Disney had envisioned, the film made only a small profit. It was also controversial, leading to the charges of racism that—along with anti-Semitism— dog Walt's reputation to this day. (*Song of the South* is the one Disney film never issued on DVD in the U.S. and remains a corporate embarrassment: Disney's elephant in the room ... one that doesn't fly.)

Walt's insensitivity—or was it naïveté?—surfaced once again in 1947, when he became a "friendly" witness before the House Un-American Activities Committee, baselessly calling the men who'd walked out on him six years before "communists."

Once again, the Disney brand was in the doldrums, dominated by pleasantly unexceptional fare such as *Fun and Fancy Free* (1947) and *Melody Time* (1948). Damning with faint praise, LIFE called the second half of 1949's *The Adventures of Ichabod and Mr. Toad* "good enough to convince Disney admirers that the old master can still display all the bounce and vitality that he had before the war." Though the great Soviet filmmaker Sergey Eisenstein thought 1946's

Make Mine Music was "absolutely ingenious," Walt knew the work wasn't his best.

There were a few high points— commercially, at least—in the years that followed. In 1948, a faked live-action documentary, *Seal Island*, became the first in a successful series of True-Life Adventures. And 1950's *Cinderella* was an unexpected hit. But Walt could only see what was wrong with it, mostly flaws resulting from cutting corners. He said he would never make anything as good as *Snow White*, according to biographer Neal Gabler—even though his focus wasn't on the movies anymore.

Instead, he had become preoccupied with trains.

A New Beginning

How Walt's obsession with toy trains—inspired Disneyland . . . and the television shows that paid for it

••

WALT ACTING LIKE the excited little boy he often was—even in his fifties—before Sleeping Beauty Castle during ABC's live broadcast of Disneyland's opening day. The event was a disaster. When the TV show's director asked an art director what he could shoot in the unfinished Tomorrowland, he was told, "We're going to be pouring cement." But Walt was typically undaunted, saying, "We have a lot of work to do— let's fix it all."

WALT INCREASINGLY lost interest in his studio's films as he became obsessed with Disneyland, but many first-rate (and profitable) movies were produced during these years—among them 1955's *Lady and the Tramp*. Here, the Mello Men—a popular singing quartet that frequently worked for Disney, not to mention Elvis Presley—record the barks and howls that become a kind of canine barbershop quartet in the popular film.

*"I am not Walt Disney . . .
Walt Disney doesn't smoke.
I smoke. Walt Disney
doesn't drink. I drink."*

—WALT DISNEY

On December 8, 1947, Walt wrote a letter to his sister: "I bought myself a birthday-Christmas present—something I've wanted all my life—an electric train! . . . It's a freight train with a whistle, and real smoke comes out of the smokestack—there are switches, semaphores, stations, and everything! It's just wonderful!"

Walt had always been fascinated by trains—they were part of his Marceline mythos—but in his late forties he became obsessed. As others oversaw Disney films of the period (including *Lady and the Tramp, Sleeping Beauty,* and *20,000 Leagues Under the Sea,* all shown on these pages), Walt supervised engineers in the construction of his own custom scale-model locomotive. Finally, he rolled up his sleeves and started building it himself.

In 1950, after the Disney family moved into a new home in Holmby Hills, Walt had a version of his father's Marceline barn built on the property, where it became home to what he called the Carolwood Pacific Railroad. (The train was dubbed the Lilly Belle, after his wife.) When Lillian refused to let Walt run tracks through her garden, Walt was undaunted: He decided to build a tunnel underneath. But he insisted that it be built with an S curve to deliver twisty thrills in the dark.

"Walt, it'd be a lot cheaper if you built the tunnel straight," his foreman said.

"Hell, it'd be cheaper not to do this at all," he replied.

In 1952, Lillian began to suspect that her husband's obsession was becoming much more than midlife regression. He was, she thought, planning something. He had, for starters, sold their Palm Springs vacation home, borrowed against his life insurance policy, and even sold the rights to his name. "It was one of those moments when Walt's imagination was going to take off into the wild blue yonder, and everything will explode," she said.

This time, the explosion took the form of an amusement park.

During World War II, American amusement parks were mostly tawdry affairs, with "dime-a-dance and beer halls

"WHAT THE HELL are all those birds there for anyway?" Walt asks while directing a story conference for 1959's *Sleeping Beauty*. Just above: "The prince has a medieval haircut as close as possible to a teenager's ducktail," LIFE wrote. At right: Jane Fowler modeling Maleficent. *Sleeping Beauty* cost $6 million, took six years to make, and involved 1,440 colored drawings for every minute of film, but it was a commercial disappointment.

and burlesque theaters," Jim Hillman, author of *Amusement Parks* and a director of the National Amusement Park Historical Association, tells LIFE. "Since the servicemen brought cash, a precious commodity in war years, the parks attracted an element of crime and seediness—drugs, pickpockets, even prostitutes."

When Lillian warned Walt that amusement parks "were not safe," he responded, "Mine's not going to be like that."

Though Walt initially hired an architectural firm to make the first stabs at what eventually became Disneyland, the real work was done by what he called his Imagineers (studio employees who created innovative special effects and techniques). That's because the park was, Walt said, a sort

of movie that people could step into and interact with. "No one had ever tried to tell a story in an amusement park before," longtime Disney associate Marty Sklar tells LIFE. (Now considered a "Disney Legend," Sklar was the only person involved in the opening of all 11 of the existing theme parks.) "And here Walt was inventing a whole new genre again."

But as usual Walt needed cash—and this time it came from, of all things, television.

On Christmas Day, 1950, NBC aired *One Hour in Wonderland,* Walt's first television special. Designed to promote his latest film, *Alice in Wonderland,* the show featured characters and clips from the new movie, along with old favorites like Snow White and Donald Duck. Ninety percent of people watching TV that holiday were watching Walt, and so were the critics. "Walt Disney can take over television any time he likes," the *New York Times* enthused.

Not surprisingly, he did. In 1953, Walt and Roy took their idea for a new anthology TV show called *Disneyland* to market, with the condition that the acquiring network had to invest in

ABOVE: A PROPMAN with a nine-foot wooden wrench during the filming of *20,000 Leagues Under the Sea,* shown in a 1954 LIFE story. The propmen also had to lug a carpet used to keep underwater sand from ruining the shots. At right: Actors harvest seaweed, helped by a propman with a net. "In the Caribbean, off Nassau, Bahamas, 83 actor-divers, cameramen, grips, propmen, professional salvage men, lifeguards, and directors are trying to make [the film] as authentic as possible," LIFE wrote, calling it "the greatest underwater venture in film history."

MARC WANAMAKER/BISON ARCHIVES

IN 1954, WALT TREATS his kids and their friends to a ride in his prized scale-model train. During the same period, Walt was crafting a series of three-dimensional miniature scenes of Americana—such as "Granny Kincaid's Cabin," complete with chairs, fireplace, and rug—in what he hoped would become an exhibit called Disneylandia. These two pursuits merged, becoming the catalyst for Disneyland. (Walt's obsession with making miniature models move was arguably the beginning of such attractions as Pirates of the Caribbean.)

their risky park. (The price tag: a whopping $15 million loan, in return for 35 percent ownership of Disneyland.) When the two established networks, CBS and NBC, balked, Walt and Roy approached the struggling American Broadcasting Company.

In the early 1950s, ABC was the "weak sister" of the TV triumvirate, broadcasting the likes of *Junior Press Conference* and *Boxing from Eastern Parkway* (by contrast, NBC had Milton Berle and CBS had *I Love Lucy*). "ABC needed the television show so damn bad that they bought the amusement park," Walt said.

On October 27, 1954, *Disneyland* premiered on ABC. It was an immediate hit, becoming the first ABC show to enter the Nielsen Top 10. Though the Disneys lost money on the program, it had not been designed for profit but rather as an hour-long weekly advertisement for the nascent park and upcoming films. Since Disneyland was designed to be separated into four distinct lands (Fantasyland, Adventureland, Frontierland, and Tomorrowland), every episode of *Disneyland* would reflect one of them.

The first of these iterations—inspired by Frontierland—was an unlikely smash. Premiering in December of 1954, "Davy Crockett" became a national phenomenon. "The Crockett craze, unexpected

Continued on page 68

WALT SNAPS HIS DAUGHTERS, Sharon (left) and Diane, while they pose in the garden outside their Holmby Hills home, circa 1955. Though Walt doted on his girls, the workaholic was seldom home—sometimes sleeping in his office, which had an adjoining bedroom. But having lost some interest in his studio's films, he was spending more and more time with his family—until a little something called Disneyland fired his obsessive imagination once again.

show," Sklar says. "People thought, 'I'd buy a used car from that man.' But he didn't set out to create that—it happened because he believed in what he was doing, and that came through loud and clear."

But the genial "Uncle Walt" persona was arguably as manufactured as his famous signature, which had been designed by his animators. "I'm not Walt Disney," he said. "I do a lot of things Walt Disney wouldn't do. Walt Disney doesn't smoke. I smoke. Walt Disney doesn't drink. I drink."

As "Walt Disney" grew more and more famous, the man himself became increasingly dictatorial—once again reflecting the father he had spent his life running from. "You were being patted on the head by this kindly old uncle who wanted you to be happy and have a nice warm lunch, when you suddenly realized you were talking to Attila the Hun," longtime employee Bill Walsh later said.

Adds Sklar: "Walt was not a person that you got 'atta boy' praise from. I think the way we all found out what he thought of our work was from somebody else, because he'd talk about it. And if you got another assignment, you knew he was happy with what you had done. The praise was in the product."

But as always, Walt's boyish enthusiasm was infectious, as was his desire to create a world that existed for one reason: to make people happy. Just as he used to stay for days at the studio, Walt now practically lived in his apartment above Disneyland's Main Street firehouse. At last he had found a project that he could work on until it was perfect. "When you wrap up a picture and turn it over to Technicolor, you're through," he said. "I want something live, something that would grow."

WALT AND JOHN HENCH, one of his artists, discussing plans for Disneyland, hold the map Walt called "The $5-Million Layout" (above). Says longtime Disney associate Marty Sklar: "Once, when a marketing team announced a campaign to promote the Disney parks as 'escapism,' John got so upset. He said they're not about escapism at all—they're about the reassurance that things can be done right." Opposite page: Disney becomes increasingly famous as "Uncle Walt," thanks to ABC's hit *Disneyland*.

even by the watchful Walt Disney, has produced a corresponding frenzy in commercial circles," LIFE reported in 1955, listing baby shoes, wallets, and even the "Davy Crockett Mambo" among merchandising that it estimated was worth $100 million. (One year later, another Disney TV show, *The Mickey Mouse Club*, would become a similar phenomenon.)

Though Walt had been famous since the 1930s, the TV show turned him into an icon. "There was such a public trust in Walt because of that

Continued on page 73

WALT'S BROTHER and business partner, Roy, posing with product tie-ins in 1950. Though these dolls and games and books provided a steady revenue source, they were not enough to finance Walt's latest dream: Disneyland. That money would eventually come from a uniquely synergistic television deal. (Note that this was shot by LIFE photographer Alfred Eisenstaedt, perhaps most famous for the iconic image of an American sailor kissing a young nurse in Times Square on V-J Day, August 14, 1945.)

Typically, nothing escaped his attention. "He knew where every pipe was," Lillian once said. "He knew the height of every building." He was particularly obsessed with trees, according to biographer Bob Thomas. Unlike the buildings on Main Street, which were scaled down to create a sense of control, Walt wanted his trees to be as big as possible. "Where did you get the bushes?" he asked when one employee showed him trees that weren't big enough. He even rejected a tree for being "out of character."

As usual, Walt would take advantage of cutting-edge technology. "There's an outfit in Washington called DARPA that makes military equipment available to the public when it's no longer a secret," says Sklar. "The Enchanted Tiki Room attraction was programmed and sequenced with the equipment that ran the Polaris missiles on submarines." (At the time, Tiki's control room was larger than the attraction itself, says Sklar, "though now you could do the same thing with your cell phone.")

As a 21-year-old student at UCLA, Sklar was hired by Walt to produce a Main Street newspaper a mere month before the park's opening. "Two weeks after I went to work, I had to present the concept to Walt," he says. "At first, I was amazed that he had time for this little thing that was going to be sold for 10 cents, but I soon realized that having that paper was part of the story for Walt—at the turn of the century, every town had at least one. For him, Main Street was a real place."

It was also yet another embodiment of Marceline.

Of course, Walt's ambitions led to delays. Six weeks before the premiere, Main Street wasn't paved, and Sleeping Beauty Castle wasn't finished. Plumbers told Disney that,

thanks to a strike, they couldn't make both the drinking fountains and the bathrooms work. Walt, of course, opted to fix the bathrooms. "People can buy Pepsi-Cola," he said, "but they can't pee in the street."

On July 17, 1955, the temperature in Anaheim, California, hovered around 100 degrees. But that didn't deter the masses of people desperate to visit Disneyland. The traffic was backed up for seven miles, and the lines that snaked around the park were filled with people who had been waiting since two a.m. After the gates finally opened, the park that had expected

IN 1954, "DAVY CROCKETT," a segment on Walt's new television show, *Disneyland*, became a national phenomenon. Opposite: Kids play "The Battle of the Alamo." Above: Walt with his grandson Christopher. Just as the song "Who's Afraid of the Big Bad Wolf?" had reflected American hopes during the Depression, so Davy Crockett's motto— "First be sure you're right, then go ahead"—embodied cold war attitudes. No doubt, too, revisionist games of cowboys and Indians seemed quaintly reassuring in the nuclear age.

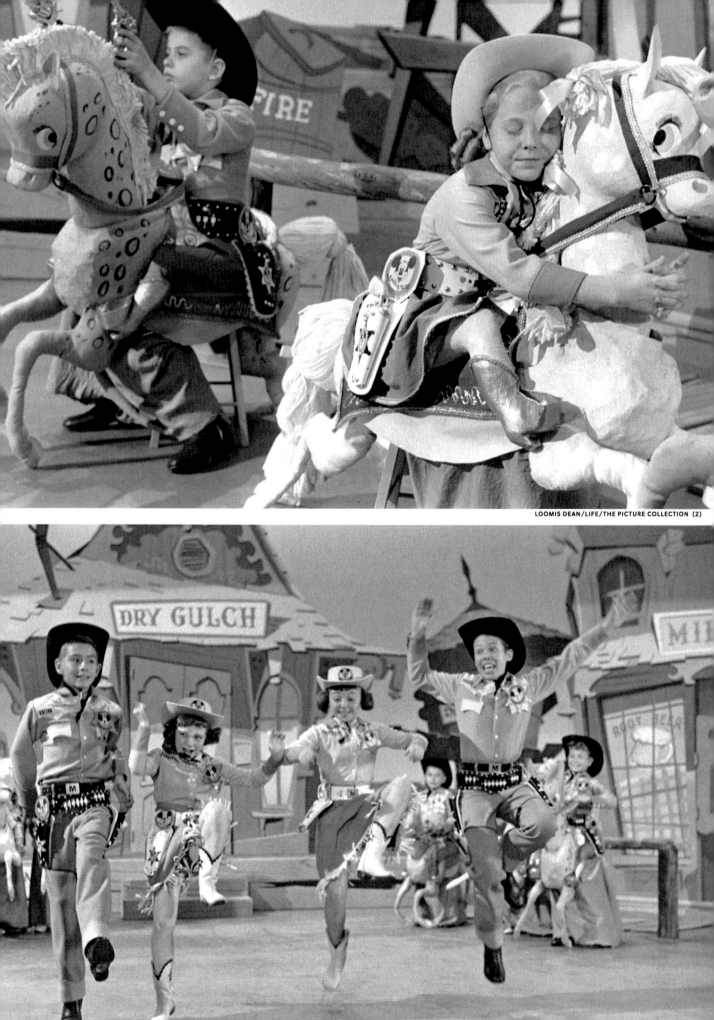

15,000 people was crammed with 28,000, many of whom had snuck in or used counterfeited tickets. "The principal problem seemed to be getting through the place," LIFE reported.

"It was," Sklar says, "a disaster."

For starters, it was so hot that women's high heels sunk into Main Street's asphalt. Mr. Toad's Wild Ride was shut down because of an electrical malfunction, and not a single Autopia car was running by the time the park closed, says Sklar: "It never dawned on them that these things had to run 12 hours a day."

Even famous guests suffered. "One of my friends happened to be on the drawbridge going into Sleeping Beauty Castle when the TV show shut everything down, because something was going on in Fantasyland," Sklar continues. "Well, it turned out that Frank Sinatra was on the drawbridge, and my associate said that he didn't remember hearing language like that anywhere before. In other words: No one got preferential treatment."

But the gaffes weren't limited to park operations. The event was documented by ABC in what had been touted as the most ambitious live TV show ever. At the outset, host Art Linkletter boasted that 29 cameras would record the festivities, but only half of them worked. At one point, Walt stared into the camera, saying, "I'd like to read these few words of dedication: A vista into a world of wondrous ideas signifying man's achievements . . ." But then he was interrupted and looked up, confused, and said, "I thought I got a signal."

The recreation revolution had been televised—badly.

But none of this mattered. Astoundingly, half the U.S. population had tuned in to the special, and one million people visited the park in its first 10 weeks. In fact, Disneyland proved so popular that, for the first time since *Snow White,* the studio was in the black. More, the park instantly became synonymous with America—a destination for people

THE MICKEY MOUSE CLUB (above and opposite) became yet another TV sensation in 1955. Strange as it may seem, Walt changed one of the show's scripts—along with some for films—to appease his friend FBI director J. Edgar Hoover, according to biographer Marc Eliot and the *New York Times.* He also gave FBI representatives access to Disneyland "for use in connection with official matters and for recreational purposes," according to an FBI document released under the Freedom of Information Act. (Walt was a secret informer for the bureau from 1940 to his death.)

DAVID F. SMITH/AP

WALT DISNEY CROSSES the drawbridge to Sleeping Beauty Castle (left) during construction in 1955. "After the war, amusement parks were seen as eyesores—dirty, morally corrupt, seedy—because they had yet to adapt to the renewal of family seen in the wholesome 1950s," says Jim Hillman, author of *Amusement Parks*. Walt, of course, was about to change all that. Below: Walt oversees the installation of the park's railroad tracks running through Main Street, U.S.A., with the castle in the background.

MARC WANAMAKER/BISON ARCHIVES

from all over the world, including not a few heads of state.

In September 1959, Soviet premier Nikita Khrushchev was touring the United States when he was told he could not visit Disneyland for security reasons, causing him to explode. "Then what must I do? Commit suicide? What is it? Is there an epidemic of cholera there or something? Or have gangsters taken hold of the place that can destroy me?"

Though Walt continued ceding control over the studio's movies, he could never completely distance himself, often meddling at the last minute—much to the consternation of the people who had been working hard all along. But nearly a decade after Disneyland opened, a little of the old cinematic spark brought Walt's focus back to the studio. One day, he took his new songwriting team of Richard and Robert Sherman

aside and asked them a question.

"He said, 'Do you know what a nanny is?'" Robert Sherman recalled. "And we said, 'Yeah, a goat.'"

In 1964, *Mary Poppins* became the studio's biggest hit since *Snow White*—and earned Walt his only Best Picture nomination. (The award went to *My Fair Lady*.)

In the mid-'60s, Walt and his team had secretly begun buying up land in central Florida for what they called Project Future. On November 15, 1965, Walt held a press conference in Orlando but was deliberately vague about his plans. When the state's governor asked, "Will it be a Disneyland?" Walt replied: "I've always said there will never be another Disneyland."

No, but there would be a Disney *World*.

Having learned lessons from his first park, Walt and his team were determined not to repeat earlier mistakes. "At Anaheim," one Disney officer later told LIFE, "we lost control of the environment." (The area surrounding the park became packed with competing, down-market hotels and restaurants.) Whereas Disneyland had occupied some 200 acres, Disney World had 27,400, and Cinderella Castle would be more than twice as tall as Sleeping Beauty Castle.

But Walt's real interest lay in the even more ambitious EPCOT, a fully functional, utopian city that would, he believed, change the way that people lived, thereby shaping civilization itself. In a nation rife with civil unrest, the ever-optimistic Walt felt that EPCOT could offer a corrective, becoming in the process his greatest achievement. "Fancy being remembered around the world for the invention of a mouse!" he exclaimed.

EPCOT was inspired in part by the installations that Disney had created for General Electric, Ford, UNICEF, and the state of Illinois in the 1964–65 New York World's Fair. Those exhibits featured Disney's first audio-animatronic figure (a moving, talking Lincoln, later featured at Disneyland) and the It's a Small World boat ride. General Electric's Disney-designed Progressland offered "a modern all-electric city and the newest advances in electrical living"—not to mention a display

CHILDREN RUN THROUGH Sleeping Beauty Castle at Disneyland in 1955, opposite. "Here, fantasy and aesthetics overtook the wild thrills and perceived—sometimes actual—danger of the existing urban parks," says Jim Hillman. "Employees were dressed to present a uniform appearance. Themed areas were kept spotless and visitors were deemed guests of the Kingdom, not just gullible customers." Above: Indians keep a lookout in Frontierland.

LOOMIS DEAN/LIFE/THE PICTURE COLLECTION

ALLAN GRANT/LIFE/THE PICTURE COLLECTION

PARK VISITORS enjoy Disneyland's *Alice in Wonderland*–themed Mad Tea Party ride, above and opposite. Though the park was ostensibly for children, plenty of adults clamored for admission—including heads of state such as India's prime minister Jawaharlal Nehru and Indonesian president Sukarno.

of thermonuclear fusion ("the secret of the sun, that may in the far-off future become man's greatest power source").

Today, in an era dominated by ecological crises, it's hard to understand the appeal of an electric city as a glorified carnival attraction. But Walt believed in the upside of technology (one *Disneyland* episode was "Our Friend the Atom"), and he saw EPCOT as a place where companies could demonstrate their latest inventions. "When he went around to see the innovations produced by different labs—RCA, IBM, GE—Walt kept asking, 'When can I buy a product with that technology?'" Sklar says. "EPCOT was focused on telling the public about new things, reflecting optimism for a better future."

Though Walt remained as restless as ever in his sixties, he was facing an inevitable decline. He had always enjoyed a Scotch mist at the end of his working day, and he would have at least one more cocktail with Lillian when he returned home—but toward the end of his life, one employee, Jack Kinney, frequently saw him driving from the studio at night, swerving. "He must have

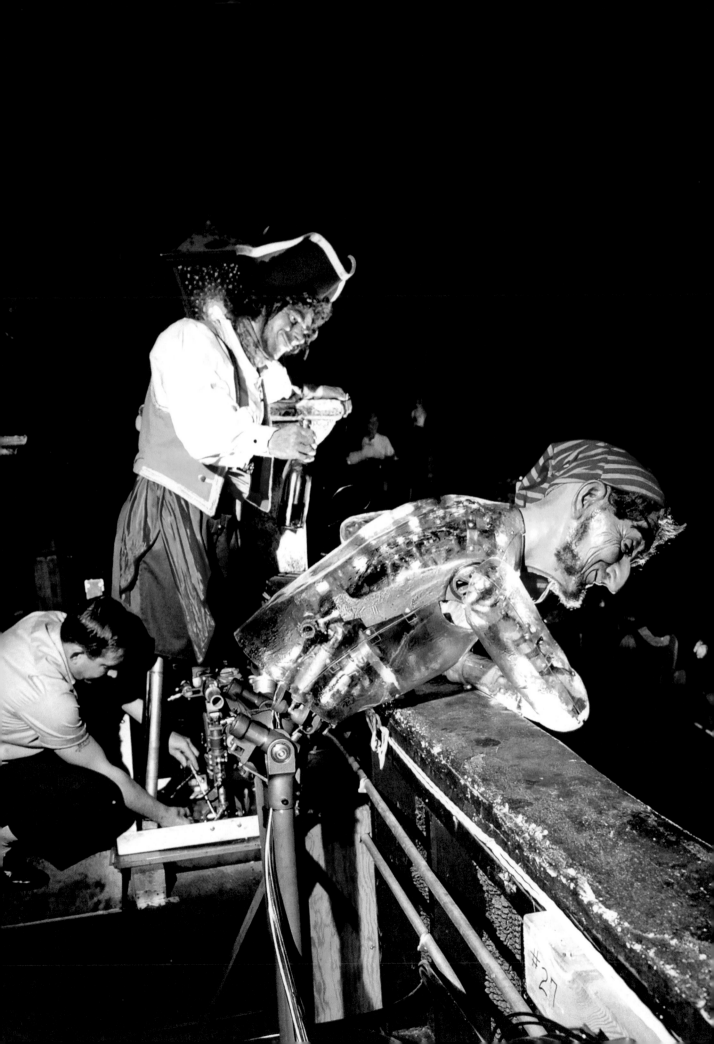

DISNEYLAND'S PIRATES of the Caribbean was the last ride Walt personally supervised. "We did a mock-up for him a few months before he passed away," says Marty Sklar, "and X Atencio [who wrote the dialogue] thought he had overwritten it—everyone was speaking at once, and he was worried you wouldn't be able to hear what they were saying. But Walt loved it. He said, 'It's like a cocktail party.'"

had someone watching over him," Kinney wrote.

The times, too, were turning against him. The war in Vietnam intensified; the Beatles hit their antic stride; and race riots erupted in urban America, but the Disney studios kept pumping out such forgettable productions as *That Darn Cat!* and *Moon Pilots*. The "Uncle Walt" who had perfectly reflected the 1950s became, as the '60s progressed, hopelessly quaint.

Walt himself became increasingly introspective. Late at night, he would sometimes tell the Sherman Brothers to "play it," meaning "Feed the Birds," the plaintive song from Mary Poppins. Though the Shermans were never sure why Walt asked for this, it almost certainly reflected the melancholy the great man felt as he approached the inevitable end.

One day, Walt did something unexpected: He told the Shermans to "Keep up the good work, fellas." Said Richard: "It was the first time, and only time, he ever complimented our work."

In November 1966, Walt checked into St. Joseph's Hospital for surgery, hoping to relieve the lingering pain from his 1930s polo injury. But doctors soon discovered a walnut-size tumor in his lungs—probably the result of a life's worth of chain-smoking unfiltered cigarettes. The growth was, not surprisingly, malignant—and had spread throughout his left lung.

After surgery, Walt soon had to *Continued on page 86*

ED WIDDIS/AP

©BUENA VISTA DISTRIBUTION COMPANY, COURTESY PHOTOFEST

ABOVE: **JULIE ANDREWS**, **left, Dick Van Dyke, and, just behind him, Walt, outside Grauman's Chinese Theatre at the world premier of** *Mary Poppins* **in 1964. "There is always something uncalculated about a truly charming movie," critic Roger Ebert later wrote. "You had the feeling . . . that the people who were making** *Mary Poppins* **didn't exactly know what they had. They knew they were having fun, but they didn't know they were striking some sort of chord millions of people would respond to." At right: Mary Poppins uses her own mode of transportation.**

be rushed back into the hospital. Though he was given perhaps two years to live, he was, as usual, planning for the future—even imagining the map of EPCOT on his hospital ceiling. "Now, there is where the highway will run," he told Roy, pointing. "And there is the route for the monorail . . ."

He had more than EPCOT on his mind, of course. "He had motion pictures in the works," says Sklar. "He had Walt Disney World; he had the idea for CalArts, a school of all the arts." But all the willpower and imagination in the world couldn't stop the disease—and on December 15, 1966, Walt Disney died.

The man with the soul of the dreamy paperboy slogging through snowy Kansas City would, of course, live on in the wishes that his heart had made and that his will had tirelessly realized. But the EPCOT Center that finally opened in 1982 bore little resemblance to Walt's Community of the Future, which Roy had quashed after Walt's death. The reason? "Walt's dead," he simply said.

WALT'S OFFICE IN 1971. Toward the end of his life, Disney had become synonymous with lightweight entertainment, but people often overlook how uncompromising his vision could be. "*Snow White* had a gothic horror quality in its darker moments," says animator and author Stephen Cavalier. "*Pinocchio* was even more gothic, while *Fantasia* featured the terrifying power of 'Night on Bald Mountain.'" Though *Dumbo* was an attempt to make a lighter, cuter film, "even that ended up containing trauma and madness and drunken hallucinations." And *Bambi* features "Disney's most gut-wrenchingly sad and violent sequences."

After Walt

How Disney's last dream died with him ... and controversial new leadership reanimated (literally) the struggling studio

— •• —

FIREWORKS BURST over Cinderella Castle in Florida's Walt Disney World. The park "incorporates some lessons learned in the original gold mine called Disneyland that opened 16 years ago at Anaheim," LIFE reported in "Disney Moves East," a 1971 cover story. Because Disneyland was relatively small, the company estimated at the time that it had lost out on $500 million that tourists spent on surrounding businesses. "Control of the environment and the moneymaking is not likely to escape again," LIFE concluded.

"*Fancy being remembered around the world for the invention of a mouse!*"
—WALT DISNEY

I n 1971, Walt Disney World Resort opened to great fanfare near Orlando. "The new site is in Florida, but the air is pure old Disney," LIFE wrote in its cover story. "Who else could be responsible for this carefully crafted vision of the American past, the intricate, hokey, hugely expensive assemblage of lives and places that never were?" The park embodied, the magazine added, "the businesslike use of fantasy, the no-nonsense approach to nonsense."

Though Walt Disney World was a massive success, in the rudderless decades that followed, the Disney company became more about real estate than innovation or creativity. "It seemed to be in the grip of 'what would Walt do?' paralysis," Kim Masters, author of *The Keys to the Kingdom* and editor-at-large at *The Hollywood Reporter,* tells LIFE. "Everybody wanted to keep things exactly the same, so of course it started to drift."

That all changed in 1984 with the arrival of CEO Michael Eisner, president Frank Wells, and chairman Jeffrey Katzenberg. Though Eisner was a volatile, controversial figure, Wells kept him in check—and Katzenberg almost single-handedly revitalized the animation division, culminating in the vast success of 1994's *The Lion King,* the highest-grossing hand-drawn animated film ever made.

But after Wells died in a helicopter crash in 1994, Eisner tangled with Steve Jobs, torpedoed a relationship with Pixar, had a falling out with Katzenberg, and fired new president Michael Ovitz, who had been in place for only 14 months, costing the company a $140 million payout. When Eisner left after his contract expired in 2006, his deputy Bob Iger got the top spot, overseeing the phenomenal success that continues to this day, fueled in part by the acquisition of Pixar, Marvel Entertainment, ESPN, ABC, and Lucasfilm (the *Star Wars* franchise).

There have been setbacks, of course. The company opened a series of controversial international parks, the first of which was Tokyo Disney Resort in 1983. "The Japanese said, 'Don't try to tell us stories about ourselves, because you can't do it,'" Sklar says. "But our chairman wanted to be sure that schoolchildren came, so he made

YURIKO NAKAO/REUTERS

A KIMONO-CLAD Minnie Mouse performs with dancers to celebrate the New Year at Tokyo DisneySea in Urayasu, near Tokyo, in 2006.

CARL DE KEYZER/MAGNUM

BOBBY YIP/REUTERS

us do a show called Meet the World, a history of Japan—and how do you tell the story of the Second World War at Disneyland in Japan? It was a disaster."

Opening in 1992, Euro Disney—located outside Paris—was also controversial. "The French basically said, 'Yes, do stories about us because we're the greatest culture in the world!'" Sklar says. "But that story was a disaster, too." The resort struggled financially, the U.K.'s *Independent* calling it "America's cultural Vietnam, a punishment for the hubristic overreach of its commercial colonisation of the globe."

But Sklar insists that Walt would be "ecstatic" about the opening of the 12th park, Shanghai Disney, scheduled for June 2016. "They spent a year traveling around China, talking to people, finding artists and designers and architects to add to the staff," he says, "so it's become a truly international project. It's beautifully designed, with a lot of new ideas based on things that Walt started in Disneyland. It's going to be fantastic."

What would Walt think about what has happened to his company in the years since his death? "I always refused to answer that question—until we opened Hong Kong Disneyland," says Sklar. "That's when I said that Walt was an impatient man—and, if he were around, he would probably say, 'What took you so long?'"

◄ EUROPEAN PRINCESSES

Ball is seen, opposite, at Disneyland Paris (formerly Euro Disney). The Disney Princess line of dolls and costumes has been the source of controversy. In the *New York Times*, author Peggy Orenstein wrote: "I watch my fellow mothers, women who once swore they'd never be dependent on a man, smile indulgently at daughters who warble 'So This Is Love' or insist on being called Snow White." Above: A young guest smiles at Hong Kong Disneyland a day before its official opening in 2005.

MICKEY MOUSE PREPARES for a date with Minnie (his girlfriend of nearly 90 years as of this writing) at EPCOT Center in Orlando in 1982.

RENÉ BURRI/MAGNUM

EDITOR/WRITER J.I. Baker
DIRECTOR OF PHOTOGRAPHY Christina Lieberman
CREATIVE DIRECTOR Mimi Park
COPY CHIEF Parlan McGaw
COPY EDITOR Joel Van Liew
PICTURE EDITOR Rachel Hatch
WRITER-REPORTERS
Amy Lennard Goehner, Daniel S. Levy
PHOTO ASSISTANT Christopher Manahan
DIRECTOR OF PHOTOGRAPHY EMERITA
Barbara Baker Burrows

TIME INC. BOOKS
PUBLISHER Margot Schupf
ASSOCIATE PUBLISHER Allison Devlin
VICE PRESIDENT, FINANCE Terri Lombardi
EXECUTIVE DIRECTOR, MARKETING SERVICES
Carol Pittard
EXECUTIVE DIRECTOR, BUSINESS DEVELOPMENT
Suzanne Albert
EXECUTIVE PUBLISHING DIRECTOR Megan Pearlman
FINANCE DIRECTOR Kevin Harrington
SALES DIRECTOR Christi Crowley
ASSOCIATE DIRECTOR OF PUBLICITY
Courtney Greenhalgh
ASSISTANT GENERAL COUNSEL Andrew Goldberg
ASSISTANT DIRECTOR, PRODUCTION
Susan Chodakiewicz

SENIOR MANAGER, SALES MARKETING
Danielle Costa
SENIOR MANAGER, CATEGORY MARKETING
Bryan Christian
BRAND MANAGER Katherine Barnet
ASSOCIATE BRAND MANAGER Krystal Venable
ASSOCIATE PROJECT MANAGER & PRODUCTION
Anna Riego
ASSOCIATE PREPRESS MANAGER Alex Voznesenskiy

EDITORIAL DIRECTOR Stephen Koepp
CREATIVE DIRECTOR Gary Stewart
DIRECTOR OF PHOTOGRAPHY Christina Lieberman
EDITORIAL OPERATIONS DIRECTOR
Jamie Roth Major
SENIOR EDITOR Alyssa Smith
ASSISTANT ART DIRECTOR Anne-Michelle Gallero
COPY CHIEF Rina Bander
ASSISTANT MANAGING EDITOR Gina Scauzillo
ASSISTANT EDITOR Courtney Mifsud

TIME INC. PREMEDIA
Richard K. Prue (Director), Richard Shaffer
(Production), Keith Aurelio, Jen Brown,
Kevin Hart, Rosalie Khan, Patricia Koh,
Marco Lau, Brian Mai, Rudi Papiri, Clara
Renauro

SPECIAL THANKS: Brad Beatson, Jeremy Biloon,
Ian Chin, Rose Cirrincione, Pat Datta,
Nicole Fisher, Alison Foster, Joan L. Garrison,
Erika Hawxhurst, Erin Hines, Kristina Jutzi,

Jean Kennedy, Seniqua Koger, Hillary Leary,
Melissa Presti, Bhavish Rai, Kate Roncinske,
Babette Ross, Dave Rozzelle, Kelsey Smith,
Larry Wicker

Vol. 16, No. 7 • April 15, 2016

"LIFE" is a registered trademark of Time Inc.

We welcome your comments and suggestions
about LIFE Books. Please write to us at:
LIFE Books, Attention: Book Editors
P.O. Box 62310, Tampa, FL 33662-2310

If you would like to order any of our hardcover
Collector's Edition books, please call us at
800-327-6388, Monday through Friday,
7 a.m.–9 p.m. Central Time